THE COCKTAIL GUIDE

First published in 2010 by New Holland Publishers
This edition published in 2021 by New Holland Publishers
Sydney

Level 1, 178 Fox Valley Road, Waroonga, 2076, Australia

newhollandpublishers.com

A record of this book is held at the National Library of Australia.

ISBN 9781760794163

Managing Director: Fiona Schultz
Publisher: Fiona Schultz
Editor: Elise James
Designer: Yolanda La Gorcé
Production Director: Arlene Gippert
Printed in China

10 9 8 7 6 5 4 3 2

Keep up with New Holland Publishers on Facebook

 facebook.com/NewHollandPublishers

@newhollandpublishers

US$16.99

Contents

Introduction

METHODS OF MIXING COCKTAILS

The four methods below are the most common processes of mixing cocktails:

1. Shake
2. Stir
3. Build
4. Blend

1. SHAKE: To shake is to mix a cocktail by shaking it in a cocktail shaker by hand. First, fill the glass part of the shaker three quarters full with ice, then pour the ingredients on top of the ice. Less expensive ingredients are usually poured before the deluxe ingredients, just in case you make a mistake! Pour the contents of the glass into the metal part of the shaker and shake vigorously for ten to fifteen seconds. Remove the glass section and using a Hawthorn strainer, strain contents into the cocktail glass. Shaking ingredients that do not mix easily with spirits is easy and practical (eg juices, egg whites, cream and sugar syrups).

Most shakers have two or three parts. In a busy bar, the cap is often temporarily misplaced. If this happens, a coaster or the inside palm of your hand is quite effective. American shakers are best.

To sample the cocktail before serving to the customer, pour a small amount into the shaker cap and using a straw check the taste.

2. STIR: To stir a cocktail is to mix the ingredients by stirring them with ice in a mixing glass and then straining them into a chilled cocktail glass. Short circular twirls are most preferred. (NB. The glass part of a shaker will do well for this.) Spirits, liqueurs and vermouths that blend easily together are mixed by this method.

3. BUILD: To build a cocktail is to mix the ingredients in the glass in which the cocktail is to be served, floating one on top of the other. Hi-ball, long fruit juice and carbonated mixed cocktails are typically built using this technique. Where possible a swizzle stick should be put into the drink to mix the ingredients after being presented to the customer. Long straws are excellent substitutes when swizzle sticks are unavailable.

4 BLEND: To blend a cocktail is to mix the ingredients using an electric blender/mixer. It is recommended to add the fruit (fresh or tinned) first. Slicing small pieces gives a smoother texture than if you add the whole fruit. Next, pour the alcohol. Ice should always be added last. This order ensures that the fruit is blended freely with the alcoholic ingredients and allows the ice to gradually mix into the beverage, chilling it. Ideally, the blender should be on for at least 20 seconds. Following this procedure will prevent ice and fruit lumps that then need to be strained.

If the blender starts to rattle and hum, ice may be obstructing the blades from spinning. Always check that the blender is clean before you start. Angostura Bitters is alcohol based which is suitable for cleaning. Fill 4 to 5 shakes with hot water, rinse and then wipe clean.

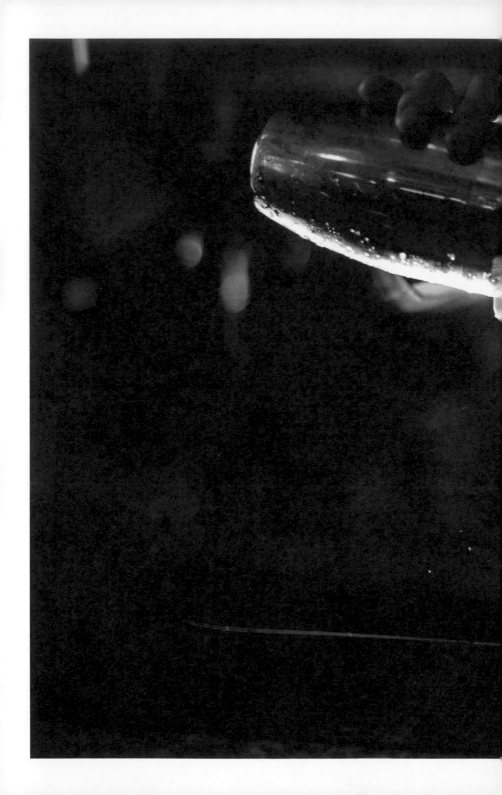

Techniques in making cocktails

1. SHAKE AND POUR: After shaking the cocktail, pour the contents straight into the glass. When pouring into highball glasses and some old fashioned glasses the ice cubes are included. This eliminates straining.

2. SHAKE AND STRAIN: Using a Hawthorn strainer (or knife) this technique prevents the ice going into the glass. Straining protects the cocktail ensuring melted ice won't dilute the mixture.

3. FLOAT INGREDIENTS: Hold the spoon right way up and rest it with the lip slightly above the level of the last layer. Fill spoon gently and the contents will flow smoothly from all around the rim. Use the back of the spoon's dish only if you are experienced.

4. FROSTING (sugar and salt rims): This technique is used to coat the rim of the glass with either salt or sugar. First, rub lemon/orange slice juice all the way around the glass rim. Next, holding the glass upside down by the stem, rest on a plate containing salt or sugar and turn slightly so that it

adheres to the glass. Pressing the glass too deeply into the salt or sugar often results in chunks sticking to the glass. A lemon slice is used for salt and an orange slice is used for sugar.

To achieve colour affects, put a small amount of grenadine or coloured liqueur in a plate and coat the rim of the glass, then gently place in the sugar. The sugar absorbs the grenadine, which turns it pink. This is much easier than mixing grenadine with sugar and then trying to get it to stick to the glass.

HELPFUL HINTS

Cocktail mixing is an art which is expressed in the preparation and presentation of the cocktail.

STORING FRUIT JUICES

Take an empty wine bottle and soak it in hot water to remove the label and sterilise the alcohol. The glass has excellent appeal and you'll find it easier to pour the correct measurement with an attached nip pourer.

SUGAR SYRUP RECIPE

Combine equal parts white sugar and boiling water, and keep stirring until the sugar is fully dissolved. Refrigerate when not in use. Putting a teaspoon of sugar into a cocktail is being lazy, it does not do the job properly as the sugar just dissolves.

JUICE TIPS

Never leave juices, coconut cream or other ingredients in cans. Pour them into clean bottles, cap and refrigerate them.

ICE

Ice is probably the most important part of cocktails. It is used in nearly all cocktails. Consequently ice must be clean and fresh at all times.

The small square cubes and flat chips of ice are superior for chilling and mixing cocktails. Ice cubes with holes are inefficient. Wet ice, ice scraps and broken ice should only be used in blenders.

CRUSHED ICE

Take the required amount of ice and fold into a clean linen cloth. Although uncivilized, the most effective method is to smash it against the bar floor. Shattering with a bottle may break the bottle. Some retailers sell portable ice crushers. Alternatively a blender may be used. Half fill with ice and then pour water into the blender until it reaches the level of the ice. Blend for about 30 seconds, strain out the water and you have perfectly crushed ice. Always try and use a metal scoop to collect the ice from the ice tray.

Never pick up the ice with your hands. This is unhygienic. Shovelling the glass into the ice tray to gather ice can also cause breakages and hence should be avoided where possible.

It is important that the ice tray is cleaned each day. As ice is colourless and odourless, many people assume wrongly it is always clean. Taking a cloth soaked in hot water, wipe the inside of the bucket.

GLASSES

Brandy balloon

Champagne flute

Coupe

Highball

Hurricane

Glass coffee cup

Champagne Flute

Margarita

Wine Glass

Highball

Brandy Balloon

Margarita

Martini glass

Old fashioned

A proven method to polishing glasses once clean is to hold each glass individually over a bucket of boiling water until the glass becomes steamy and then with a clean linen cloth rub in a circular way to ensure the glass is polished for the next serve.

Cocktails can be poured into any glass but the better the glass the better the appearance of the cocktail.

Martini   Pilsner Glass   Pint

One basic rule should apply and that is, use no coloured glasses as they spoil the appearance of cocktails. All glasses have been designed for a specific task, eg.,

1. Highball glasses for long cool refreshing drinks.

2. Martini glasses for short, sharp, or stronger drinks.

3. Champagne saucers for creamy after-dinner style drinks, etc.

The stem of the glass has been designed so you may hold it whilst polishing, leaving the bowl free of marks and germs so that you may enjoy your drink. All cocktail glasses should be kept in a refrigerator or filled with ice while you are preparing the cocktails in order to chill the glass. An appealing affect on a 90ml cocktail glass can be achieved by running the glass under cold water and then placing it in the freezer.

GARNISHES AND JUICES

Almonds	Chocolate flakes
Apple juice	Cinnamon
Apricot conserve	Cocktail onions
Banana	Coconut cream
Blueberries	Cream
Carbonated water	Crushed Pineapple
Celery	Cucumber
Celery salt	Edible flowers

Eggs	Pineapple juice
Jelly Babies	Red cocktail onions
Lemon juice	Red maraschino cherries
Lemons	Rockmelon
Lime juice	Salt
Limes	Strawberries
Milk	Sugar
Mint leaves	Sugar cubes
Nutmeg	Sugar syrup
Olives	Tabasco sauce
Orange and mango juice	Tinned fruit/pulps
Orange juice	Tinned nectars
Oranges	Tomato
Pepper	Vanilla ice cream
Pineapple	Worcestershire sauce

Simplicity is the most important fact to keep in mind when garnishing cocktails. Do not overdo the garnish; make it striking, but if you can't get near the cocktail to drink it then you have failed. Most world champion cocktails just have a lemon slice, or a single red cherry.

Tall refreshing highballs tend to have more garnish as the glass is larger. A swizzle stick should nearly always be served in long cocktails. Plastic animals, umbrellas, fans and a whole variety of novelty goods are now available to garnish with, and they add a lot of fun to the drink.

ALCOHOL RECOMMENDED FOR A COCKTAIL BAR

SPIRITS

Bourbon	Pernod
Brandy	Rum
Campari	Scotch
Canadian club	Southern comfort
Gin	Tennessee whisky
Malibu	Tequila
Ouzo	Vodka

LIQUEURS

Advocaat	Cassis
Amaretto	Chartreuse – green and yellow
Bailey's Irish cream	Cherry advocaat
Banana liqueur	Cherry brandy
Benedictine	Clayton's tonic (Non-alcoholic)
Blue curaçao	Coconut liqueur

Cointreau	Kirsch
Crème de café	Mango liqueur
Crème de menthe – green	Melon liqueur
Dark crème de cacao	Pimm's
Drambuie	Sambuca – clear
Frangelico	Sambuca – black
Galliano	Strawberry liqueur
Grand Marnier	Triple Sec
Kahlúa	

VERMOUTH

Cinzano Bianco Martini Bianco

Cinzano Dry Martini Dry

Cinzano Rosso Martini Rosso

ESSENTIAL EQUIPMENT FOR A COCKTAIL BAR

Bottle openers	Mixing glass
Knife, cutting board	Cocktail shaker
Can-opener	Electric blender
Measures (jiggers)	Free pourers
Coasters and serviettes	Scooper spoon (long teaspoon)

Hand cloths for cleaning glasses

Swizzle sticks, straws

Ice bucket

Spoon with muddler

Waiter's friend corkscrew

Hawthorn strainer

Ice scoop

DESCRIPTION OF LIQUEURS AND SPIRITS

Advocaat: A combination of fresh egg whites, yolks, sugar, brandy, vanilla and spirit. Limited shelf life. Recommended shelf life 12–15 months from date of manufacture.

Amaretto: A rich subtle liqueur with a unique almond taste.

Angostura Bitters: An essential part of any bar or kitchen. A unique additive whose origins date back to 1824. A mysterious blend of natural herbs and spices, it is a seasoning agent in both sweet and savoury dishes and drinks. Ideal for dieters as it is low in sodium and calories.

Bailey's Irish Cream: The largest selling liqueur in the world. It is a blend of Irish whisky, softened by Irish cream. It is a natural product.

Banana Liqueur: Fresh ripe bananas are the perfect base for the definitive daiquiri and a host of other exciting fruit cocktails.

Benedictine: A perfect end to a perfect meal. Serve straight, with ice, soda, or as part of a favourite cocktail.

Bourbon: Has a smooth, deep, easy taste.

Brandy: Smooth and mild spirit, is considered very smooth and palatable, ideal for mixing.

Campari: A drink for many occasions, both as a long or short drink, or as a key ingredient in many fashionable cocktails.

Cassis: Deep, rich purple promises and delivers a regal and robust taste and aroma. Cassis lends itself to neat drinking or an endless array of delicious sauces and desserts.

Chartreuse: A liqueur available in either yellow or green colour. Made by the monks of the Carthusian order. The only world famous liqueur still made by monks.

Cherry Advocaat: Same as Advocaat, infused with natural cherry.

Cherry Brandy: Is made from concentrated, morello cherry juice. Small quantity of bitter almonds and vanilla is added to make it more enjoyable as a neat drink before or after dinner. Excellent for mixers, topping, ice cream, fruit salads, pancakes, etc.

Coconut Liqueur: A smooth liqueur, composed of exotic coconut, heightened with light-bodied white rum.

Cointreau: Made from a neutral grain spirit, as opposed to cognac. An aromatic taste of natural citrus fruits. A great mixer or delightful over ice.

Crème de cacao – dark: Rich, deep chocolate. Smooth and classy. Serve on its own, or mix for all kinds of delectable treats.

Crème de cacao – white: This liqueur delivers a powerfully lively, full bodied chocolate taste. Excellent ingredient when absence of colour is desired.

Crème de menthe – green: Clear peppermint flavour, reminiscent of a fresh, crisp, clean winter's day in the mountains. Excellent mixer, a necessity in the gourmet kitchen.

Crème de menthe – white: As Crème de menthe – green, when colour is not desired.

Curaçao – blue: Same as Triple Sec, brilliant blue colour is added to make some cocktails more exciting.

Curaçao – orange: Again, same as above, but stronger in orange, colouring is used for other varieties of cocktail mixers.

Curaçao Triple Sec: Based on natural citrus fruits. Well known fact is citrus fruits are the most important aromatic taste constituents. As a liqueur one of the most versatile. Can be enjoyed with or without ice as a neat drink, or used in mixed cocktails more than any other liqueur. Triple Sec – also known as white curaçao.

Galliano – vanilla: The distinguished taste! A classic liqueur that blends with a vast array of mixed drinks.

Gin: Its aroma comes from using the highest quality juniper berries and other rare and subtle herbs. Perfect mixer for both short and long drinks.

Kirsch: A fruit brandy distilled from morello cherries. Delicious drunk straight and excellent in a variety of food recipes.

Drambuie. A Scotch whisky liqueur. Made from a secret recipe dating back to 1745. "Dram Buidheach" the drink that satisfies.

Frangelico: A precious liqueur imported from Italy. Made from wild hazelnuts with infusions of berries and flowers to enrich the taste.

Grand Marnier: An original blend of fine old cognac and an extract of oranges. The recipe is over 150 years old.

Kahlúa: A smooth, dark liqueur made from real coffee and fine clear spirits. Its origins are based in Mexico.

Malibu: A clear liqueur based on white rum with the subtle addition of coconut. Its distinctive taste blends naturally with virtually every mixer available.

Melon Liqueur: Soft green, exudes freshness. Refreshing and mouth- watering honeydew melon. Simple yet complex. Smooth on the palate, serve on the rocks, or use to create summertime cocktails.

Ouzo: The traditional spirit aperitif of Greece. The distinctive taste is derived mainly from the seed of the anise plant. A neutral grain spirit.

Peach Schnapps: Crystal clear, light liqueur, bursting with the taste of ripe peaches. Drink chilled, on the rocks or mix with any soft drink or juice.

Rum: A smooth, dry, light bodied rum, especially suited for drinks in which you require subtle aroma and delicate taste.

Rye Whiskey: Distilled from corn, rye and malted barley. A light, mild and delicate whiskey, ideal for drinking straight or in mixed cocktails.

Sambuca – clear: The Italian electric taste experience. Made from elder berries with a touch of anise.

Sambuca – black: An exciting encounter between Sambuca di Galliano and extracts of black elderberry.

Scotch Whisky: A whisky made in Scotland based on malt or grain. Similar taste to bourbon but with an added bite.

Southern Comfort: A liqueur not a bourbon as often thought. It is a unique, full-bodied liqueur with a touch of sweetness. Its recipe is a secret, but it is known to be based on peaches and apricots.

Strawberry Liqueur: Fluorescent red, unmistakable strawberry bouquet. Natural liqueur delivers a true to nature, fresh strawberry taste.

Tennessee Whiskey : Contrary to popular belief, this is not a bourbon, it is a distinctive product called Tennessee Whiskey. Made from the 'old sour mash' process. Leached through hard maple charcoal, then aged in charred white oak barrels, at a controlled temperature, acquiring body, bouquet and colour, yet remaining smooth.

Tequila: Distilled from the Mexcal variety of the cacti plant. A perfect mixer or drink straight with salt and lemon.

Tia Maria: A liqueur with a cane spirit base, and its taste derived from the finest Jamaican coffee. It is not too sweet with a subtle taste of coffee.

Vermouth: By description, vermouth is a herbally infused wine.

Three styles are most prevalent, these are:

Rosso: A bitter sweet herbal taste, often drunk as an aperitif.

Bianco: Is light, fruity and refreshing. Mixes well with soda, lemonade and fruit juices.

Dry: Is crisp, light and dry and is used as a base for many cocktails.

Vodka: The second largest selling spirit in the world. Most vodkas are steeped in tanks containing charcoal, removing all odours and impurities, making a superior quality product

Triple Sec: See Blue Curaçao.

Blend

Frosty bliss ... the perfect
accompaniment to a warm
summer's day.

Piña Colada

Glass: hurricane
Garnish: maraschino cherry and slice of fresh pineapple

> 60 ml (2 oz) light rum
> 60 ml (2 oz) pineapple juice
> 60 ml (2 oz) coconut cream (chilled)

Pour rum, juice and coconut cream into a blender over a large amount of crushed ice. Blend until slushy and pour into a chilled hurricane glass. Garnish with a maraschino cherry and a slice of pineapple then serve with a straw.

This drink may also be prepared in a cocktail shaker over a large amount of crushed ice if preferred.

VARIATIONS:
Strawberry Colada: replace half the rum with strawberry liqueur, and add two diced fresh strawberries before blending

Banana Colada: replace half the rum with banana liqueur and add half a banana before blending

Tropicolada: replace half the rum with 15 ml (1/2 fl oz) Midori and 15 ml (1/2 fl oz) of banana liqueur. Sprinkle with grated coconut after garnishing

Raspberry Colada: replace half the rum with Chambord

Amaretto Colada: replace half the rum with Amaretto

Blue Colada: replace half the rum with blue Curaçao

St. Martin Colada: replace the light rum with 30 ml (1 fl oz) spiced rum and 30 ml (1 fl oz) coconut liqueur

Frozen Daiquiri

Glass: coupe
Garnish: lime wheel

> 60 ml (2 fl oz) Bacardi
> 45 ml (1 1/2 fl oz) lime juice
> 30 ml (1 fl oz) sugar syrup

Pour ingredients over a two handfuls of crushed ice and blend until smooth then pour into chilled glass.

> Sometimes the taste of this drink can be diluted by blending it over ice. For a more intense drink, try using either a dark rum or a dark sugar syrup.

VARIATIONS:

Strawberry Daiquiri: replace half the rum with 15 ml (1/2 fl oz) Cointreau and 15 ml (1/2 fl oz) strawberry liqueur, and add 4 fresh strawberries before blending

Mango Daiquiri: replace half the rum with 15 ml (1/2 fl oz) Cointreau and 15 ml (1/2 fl oz) mango liqueur, and add half a diced fresh mango before blending

Blue Daiquiri: replace a quarter of the rum with 15 ml (1/2 fl oz) blue Curaçao

Banana Daiquiri: replace a quarter of the rum with 15 ml (1/2 fl oz) banana liqueur, and add half a diced banana before blending

Daiquiri Nacional: replace half the rum with 30 ml (1 fl oz) apricot brandy and reduce the sugar syrup by half

Peach Daiquiri: replace half the rum with 15 ml (1/2 fl oz) Cointreau and 15 ml (1/2 fl oz) peach liqueur, and add a diced fresh peach before blending

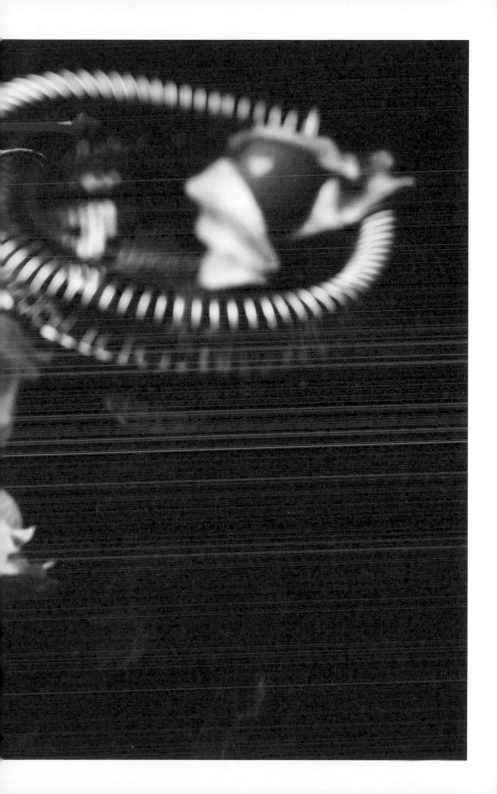

Almond Orange Frost

Glass: Coupe
Garnish: Orange slice

15 ml (1/2 fl oz) Amaretto
15 ml (1/2 fl oz) Frangelico
15 ml (1/2 fl oz) Chambord
10 ml (1/3 fl oz) fresh lime juice
10 ml (1/3 fl oz) fresh lemon juice
2 scoops orange sorbet

Add ingredients to a small amount of crushed ice and blend.

For an interesting variation to this recipe, try different sorbet flavours.
You are only limited by your imagination!

Bananarama

Glass: large martini
Garnish: two banana slices wedged on rim of glass

30 ml (1 fl oz) vodka
30 ml (1 fl oz) Kahlúa
15 ml (1 fl oz) Bailey's Irish Cream
1 banana
60 ml (2 fl oz) cream

Blend with ice.

Chiquita

Glass: small hurricane
Garnish: banana slices on rim of glass

45 ml (1½ fl oz) vodka
10 ml (1/3 fl oz) banana liqueur
10 ml (1/3 fl oz) lime juice
half a sliced banana
pinch of sugar
bitter lemon, to top

Blend with ice and pour. Top with bitter lemon.

El Burro

Glass: martini
Garnish: banana slices on rim of glass

15 ml (½ fl oz) Kahlúa
15 ml (½ fl oz) rum
30 ml (1 fl oz) coconut cream
30 ml (1 fl oz) cream
1/2 banana

Add ingredients to a small amount of crushed ice and blend.

Gomango

Glass: large hurricane
Garnish: Butterflied strawberry on side of glass

> 15 ml (1/2 fl oz) triple sec
> 15 ml (1/2 fl oz) crème de cacao
> 15 ml (1/2 fl oz) cherry advocaat
> 15 ml (1/2 fl oz) orange juice
> 15 ml (1/2 fl oz) cream
> 1 cheek of fresh mango

Add ingredients to blender over crushed ice and blend until smooth.

Kelly's Comfort

Glass: highball
Garnish: a strawberry

> 30 ml (1 fl oz) Southern Comfort
> 30 ml (1 fl oz) Bailey's Irish Cream
> 30 ml (1 fl oz) milk
> 4 strawberries
> 15 ml sugar syrup

Add ingredients to blender over crushed ice and blend until smooth.

Lady M

Glass: small hurricane
Garnish: strawberry on side of glass sprinkled with grated chocolate

45 ml (1 1/2 fl oz) Frangelico
45 ml (1 1/2 fl oz) melon liqueur
2 scoops vanilla ice cream

Blend for more than 20 seconds to thoroughly mix ingredients.

Malibu Magic

Glass: small hurricane
Garnish: a single strawberry and twisted orange peel

30 ml (1 fl oz) Malibu*
30 ml (1 fl oz) strawberry liqueur
30 ml (1 fl oz) orange juice
3–4 fresh strawberries
60 ml (2 fl oz) cream

Add ingredients to blender over crushed ice and blend until smooth.

Frozen Margarita

Glass: margarita

60 ml (2 fl oz) tequila
30 ml (1 fl oz) lime juice
15 ml (1/2 fl oz) Cointreau

Add ingredients to blender over crushed ice and blend until smooth.

Midori Avalanche

Glass: hurricane
Garnish: triangle of pineapple on side of glass

30 ml (1 fl oz) blue curaçao
30 ml (1 fl oz)Midori
15 ml (1/2 fl oz) triple sec
60 ml (2 fl oz) pineapple juice

Pour blue curaçao into glass. Blend other ingredients with ice and pour.

Be sure to use plenty of ice to quench a hot dry thirst.

Palm Sundae

Glass: hurricane glass
Garnish: orange wedge, pineapple leaves and maraschino cherry

45 ml (1 1/2 fl oz) peach liqueur
30 ml(1 fl oz) coconut liqueur
15 ml (1/2 fl oz) banana liqueur
60 ml (2 fl oz) tropical fruit juice
3 fresh strawberries

Add ingredients to blender over crushed ice and blend until smooth.

Polynesia

Glass: champagne flute
Garnish: banana slice

30 ml (1 fl oz) white rum
30 ml (1 fl oz) melon liqueur
10 ml (1/3 fl oz) lime juice
1/2 egg white

Add ingredients to blender over crushed ice and blend until smooth.

Pretty Woman

Glass: hurricane
Garnish: Pineapple and umbrella on side of glass

Blender 1

30 ml (1 fl oz) melon liqueur
30 ml (1 fl oz) Malibu

Blender 2

30 ml (1 fl oz) strawberry liqueur
3–4 strawberries

Blend with ice in two separate blenders and pour.

Remember to tilt the glass when pouring the two sets of ingredients into the glass. Choosing a long glass will assist you. Very alcoholic as there is no juice. A kaleidoscope of colour for you to enjoy.

Satin Pillow

Glass: martini
Garnish: cut a strawberry in half and place on side of glass then swirl cream over strawberry halves

1 teaspoon strawberry liqueur
10 ml (1/3 fl oz) Cointreau
15 ml (1/2 fl oz) Frangelico
15 ml (1/2 fl oz) Tia Maria
20 ml (2/3 fl oz) pineapple juice
20 ml (2/3 fl oz) cream

Add ingredients to blender over crushed ice and blend until smooth.

For extra flavour add a couple of fresh or frozen strawberries to the mixture before blending.

Scorpion

Glass: martini
Garnish: halved strawberry and orange peel

> 15 ml (1/2 fl oz) dark rum
> 15 ml (1/2 fl oz) cognac
> 15 ml (1/2 fl oz) Sambuca
> 15 ml (1/2 fl oz) orgeat syrup
> 45 ml (1 1/2 fl oz) orange juice
> 15 ml (1/2 fl oz) lemon juice

Blend with ice.

The trading capital of the Middle East is where this perilous animal and cocktail comes from! Remember they have a sting in their tail. Orgeat is an almond-flavoured non-alcoholic syrup. Amaretto may be used as a substitute.

Summer Breeze

Glass: hurricane
Garnish: half an orange slice and orange peel twist

> 60 ml (2 fl oz) peach liqueur
> 15 ml (1/2 fl oz) rum
> 15 ml (1/2 fl oz) mango liqueur
> 15 ml (1/2 fl oz) gin
> 60 ml (2 fl oz) pineapple juice
> 60 ml (2 fl oz) orange juice
> 1 fresh mango
> 1 fresh peach

Add ingredients to blender over crushed ice and blend until smooth.

Build

Quick and easy
– and sometimes quite potent!

Americano

Glass: old fashioned
Garnish: orange wedge

> 30 ml (1 fl oz) Campari
> 30 ml (1 fl oz) rosso vermouth
> soda water, to top

Build over ice and top up with soda water.

Originated from European travellers visiting America desiring a taste of European aperitifs.

Aqua Thunder

Glass: highball
Garnish: orange wedge

10 ml (1/3 fl oz) blue curaçao
10 ml (1/3 fl oz) banana liqueur
30 ml (1 fl oz) melon liqueur
10 ml (1/3 fl oz) freshly squeezed lemon
soda water, to top

Build over ice.

Watch in wonder as the soda water waterfall
splashes over the ice creating a thunderous
aqua-coloured spectacular.

Iceberg

Glass: highball
Garnish: lemon wedge

> 30 ml (1 fl oz) Absolut Citron
> 15 ml (1/2 fl oz) triple sec
> 150 ml (5 fl oz) bitter lemon

Pour Absolut Citron and triple sec over ice into a chilled highball glass and top with Bitter Lemon.

For a dramatic flair, add a couple of drops of Grenadine to the finished drink.

Australian Gold

Glass: highball
Garnish: pineapple wedge

> 30 ml (1 fl oz) rum
> 30 ml (1 fl oz) mango liqueur
> 30 ml (1 fl oz) vanilla Galliano

Build over ice.

For a more tropical flavour, try adding different fruits to the ice before you build the spirits, such as pineapple, mango and papaya.

Bellini

Glass: champagne flute
Garnish: none

45 ml (1 1/2 fl oz) peach purée
sparkling wine, to top

Pour puree into glass and add sparkling, stirring gently.

This drink is traditionally made using white peaches.

B & B

Glass: brandy balloon
Garnish: none

> 30 ml (1 fl oz) cognac
> 30 ml (1 fl oz) Benedictine

Build, no ice.

Tempt your pallet with this historical blend of choice liqueurs. Ideal with coffee.

Black Russian

Glass: old fashioned
Garnish: none

30 ml (1 fl oz) vodka
30 ml (1 fl oz) Kahlúa

Build over ice.

Many people add cola to this drink and serve it in a highball glass.

Variation:
Black Pearl: replace the Kahlúa with Tia Maria or dark crème de cacao.

Blue French

Glass: highball
Garnish: lemon slice and swizzle stick

> 30 ml (1 fl oz) pernod
> 10 ml (1/3 fl oz) blue curaçao
> 1 teaspoon lemon juice
> bitter lemon, to top

Build over ice and stir.

This cocktail can also be built over finely crushed ice for an amazing visual effect!

Champagne Cocktail

Glass: champagne flute
Garnish: strawberry on rim of glass

1 sugar cube
6 drops of Angostura bitters
15 ml (½ fl oz) cognac or brandy
champagne, to top

In the flute, soak sugar cube in Angostura bitters, before adding brandy, then top with champagne.

Dating back to the mid 1800s this is one of the most enduring and widely known classic cocktails.

Death in the Afternoon

Glass: champagne flute
Garnish: no garnish

15 ml (1/2 fl oz) Pernod
sparkling wine, to top

Build, no ice.

Depth Charger

Glass: pint glass, plus shot glass
Garnish: no garnish

1 bottle/can of beer
30 ml (1 fl oz) vodka or tequila

Fill glass with beer 3–5 centimetres below the glass rim.
Toast by touching liqueur glasses filled with spirit before
sliding into the beer glass and knocking back.

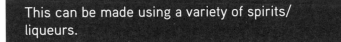

This can be made using a variety of spirits/
liqueurs.

Dubonnet Cocktail

Glass: old fashioned
Garnish: orange twist

30 ml (1 fl oz) Dubonnet
15 ml (½ fl oz) gin
1 dash orange bitters

Build and serve with or without ice.

Freddy Fudpucker

Glass: highball
Garnish: orange slice and cherry

30 ml (1 fl oz) tequila
120 ml (4 fl oz) orange juice
15 ml (1/2 fl oz) vanilla Galliano

Build over ice, making sure to float the vanilla Galliano on top of the tequila/orange juice mix.

Georgia Peach

Glass: highball
Garnish: peach or lime slice

> 30 ml (1 fl oz) Bacardi
> 30 ml (1 fl oz) peach liqueur
> 90 ml (fl oz) cranberry juice

Build over ice.

By making sure the glass is completely full of ice before building, and gently pouring ingredients in the order listed above you can create a stunning bi-colored cocktail.

God Father

Glass: old fashioned
Garnish: none

30 ml (1 fl oz) Scotch whisky
30 ml (1 fl oz) Amaretto

Build over ice.

This recipe is 'related' to the God Daughter (page 150). Both use amaretto as a flavor base.

Harvey Wallbanger

Glass: highball
Garnish: orange slice and cherry

> 45 ml (1 1/2 fl oz) vodka
> 125 ml (4 fl oz) orange juice
> 15 ml (1/2 fl oz) vanilla Galliano

Add vodka and orange juice to glass full of ice and stir. Float Galliano on top of mix and serve.

Hawaiian bartenders will tell you a visiting Irishman called Harvey pin-balled down the corridor to hotel room after a night out. Hence, he was known as "Harvey Wallbanger".

Irish Coffee

Glass: glass coffee mug
Garnish: chocolate flake optional

30 ml (1 fl oz) Irish whiskey
1 teaspoon brown sugar
hot black coffee, to top
fresh whipped cream

Dissolve brown sugar in whiskey, and top with hot coffee.
Float whipped cream on top.

Variations:

French Coffee: replace whiskey with brandy

English Coffee: replace whiskey with gin

Russian Coffee: replace whiskey with vodka

American Coffee: replace whiskey with bourbon

Calypso Coffee: replace whiskey with dark rum

Jamaican Coffee: replace whiskey with Tia Maria

Parisienne Coffee: replace whiskey with Grand Marnier

Mexican Coffee: replace whiskey with Kahlúa

Monks Coffee: replace whiskey with Benedictine

Scottish Coffee: relace whiskey with Scotch Whisky

Canadian Coffee: replace whiskey with rye

Jelly Bean

Glass: highball
Garnish: swizzle stick and straws and a red cherry dropped into glass

30 ml (1 fl oz) ouzo
15 ml (1/2 fl oz) blue curaçao
15 ml (1/2 fl oz) grenadine
top up with lemonade

Build over ice.

KGB

Glass. old fashion
Garnish: none

30 ml (1 fl oz) Kahlúa
30 ml (1 fl oz) Grand Marnier
30 ml (1 fl oz) Bailey's Irish Cream

Build over ice.

Moscow Mule

Glass: highball
Garnish: slice of lime and mint

30 ml (1 fl oz) vodka
1/2 a lime
ginger beer to top

Build over ice.

Mount Temple

Glass: martini
Garnish: dollop of cream in centre of glass

30 ml (1 fl oz) Kahlúa
30 ml (1 fl oz) tequila
30 ml (1 fl oz) coconut liqueur

Build in chilled glass.

Orgasm

Glass: old fashioned
Garnish: strawberry or cherries, optional

> 20 ml (2/3 fl oz) Bailey's Irish Cream
> 20 ml (2/3 fl oz) Cointreau

Build over ice.

A "Multiple Orgasm" is made with the addition of 30 ml (1 fl oz) of fresh cream or milk. A "Screaming Multiple Orgasm" has the addition of 15 ml (1/2 fl oz) Galliano along with 30 ml (1 fl oz) fresh cream or milk.

Pimms No. 1 Cup

Glass: highball
Garnish: orange and lemon slice, strawberry, cucumber skin, mint

> 30-45 ml (1-1 1/2 fl oz) Pimm's No. 1
> lemonade or dry ginger – or equal parts of both – to top

Build over ice.

Planter's Punch

Glass: highball
Garnish: fruit slices

45 ml (1 1/2 fl oz) dark rum
20 ml (2/3 fl oz) lemon or lime juice
30 ml (1 fl oz) orange juice
30 ml (1 fl oz) pineapple juice
1 teaspoon grenadine
10 ml grenadine
bitters, to taste
sugar syrup, to taste

Build over ice then add grenadine.

Prarie Oyster

Glass: martini
Garnish: none

30 ml (1 fl oz) brandy
salt and pepper
Worcestershire sauce
Tabasco sauce
1 egg yolk

Build, making sure not to break the egg yolk.

Red Eye

Glass: beer glass
Garnish: none

> 200 ml (7 fl oz) beer
> 90 ml (3 fl oz) tomato juice
> salt to taste

Build no ice.

This cocktail can also be done in the style of
a Bloody Mary by adding ingredients such as
Tabasco, Worcestershire sauce and celery salt.

Rocket Fuel

Glass: old fashion
Garnish: swizzle stick

> 15 ml (1/2 fl oz) rum
> 15 ml (1/2 fl oz) dry gin
> 15 ml (1/2 fl oz) vodka
> 60 ml (2 fl oz) lemonade
> 15 ml (1/2 fl oz) tequila

Build over ice.

A variation of the classic Long Island iced tea.
Try using different sodas (cola, bitter lemon) to
find the perfect rocket fuel for you!

Rusty Nail

Glass: old fashion
Garnish: lemon twist (optional)

> 30 ml (1 fl oz) Scotch whisky
> 30 ml (1 fl oz) Drambuie

Build over ice.

Hailing from the highlands of Scotland, Drambuie will raise your spirit above the centre of the world. Lemon will diffuse the bite of the Scotch.

Salty Dog

Glass: highball
Garnish: grapefruit slice

45 ml (1 1/2 fl oz) vodka
grapefruit juice, to top

Build over ice.

Straws are generally unnecessary, drink the
cocktail from the salt rim.

Screwdriver

Glass: old fashioned
Garnish: Orange twist or spiral.

45 ml (1 1/2 fl oz) vodka
45 ml (1 1/2 fl oz) orange juice

Build over ice.

Variations:
A Comfortable Screw: made with 30 ml (1 fl oz) vodka, 15 ml (1/2 fl oz) Southern Comfort and topped with orange juice.

A Slow Comfortable Screw: made with the addition of 15 ml (1/2 fl oz) sloe gin.

A Long Slow Comfortable Screw: a longer drink served in a highball glass and topped with orange juice.

A Long Slow Comfortable Screw Up Against A Wall: add of 15 ml (1/2 fl oz) Galliano floated on top of the drink.

Sex on the Beach

Glass: hurricane
Garnish: orange slice and cherry

> 30 ml (1 fl oz) vodka
> 30 ml (1 fl oz) peach schnapps
> 60 ml (2 fl oz) cranberry juice
> 60 ml (2 fl oz) orange juice.

Build over ice.

Adding the cranberry juice last will give the drink a beautiful swirling effect.

Sicilian Kiss

Glass: old fashioned
Garnish: none

30 ml Southern Comfort
30 ml Amaretto

Build with ice.

Turn this into a tall drink with the addition of
either soda, lemonade or cola.

South Pacific

Glass: highball
Garnish: lemon slice and cherry, swizzle stick and straws

30 ml dry gin
15 ml (1/2 fl oz) vanilla Galliano
top with lemonade
15 ml (1/2 fl oz) blue curaçao

Build over ice, then add the blue curaçao last.

Spritzer

Glass: wine glass
Garnish: fruit, mint, or none

dry white wine, chilled
soda water, to top

Build, no ice.

Strawberry Blonde

Glass: highball
Garnish: a red cherry

> 30 ml dark crème de cacao
> top up with cola
> fresh cream
> splash of grenadine

Build over ice, floating the cream on top.

Tequila Sunrise

Glass: highball
Garnish: orange wheel, a red cherry.

> 30 ml tequila
> 1 teaspoon grenadine
> orange juice, to top

Build over ice.

To obtain the cleanest visual effect, drop grenadine down the inside of the glass, after topping up with orange juice. Dropping grenadine in the middle creates a fallout effect, detracting from the presentation of the cocktail. Best served with chilled, freshly squeezed orange juice.

Variation:
Vodka Sunrise: replace tequila with vodka.

Tropical Itch

Glass: large hurricane glass
Garnish: Pineapple spear, mint and cherry

45 ml (1 1/2 fl oz) rum
45 ml (1 1/2 fl oz) bourbon
juice of half lime
dash Angostura bitters
pineapple juice and passionfruit, to top
30 ml (1 fl oz) dark rum

Build over ice, and float dark rum on top.

Shake

Chill, aerate and dilute ...
and look impressive as you do it!

Daiquiri Cocktail

(Frozen Daiquiri recipes can be found in the 'blend' section of this book)

Glass: coupe
Garnish: lime wheel

> **60 ml (2 oz) Bacardi**
> **30 ml (1 oz) fresh lime juice**
> **1-2 teaspoon sugar syrup**

Pour ingredients into a cocktail shaker over ice and shake. Strain into chilled glass.

Variations:
Galliano Daiquiri: replace half the Bacardi with vanilla Galliano.

Acapulco

Glass: old-fashioned
Garnish: partially torn mint leaves

> **30 ml (1 fl oz) Bacardi**
> **10 ml (1/3 fl oz) Cointreau**
> **1 egg white**
> **15 ml (1/2 fl oz) fresh lime juice**
> **sugar syrup, to taste**

Add ingredients to shaker and shake vigorously for 10-15 seconds without ice. Add ice to shaker and shake. Double strain into a chilled glass.

Cosmopolitan

Glass: martini
Garnish: orange twist

45 ml (1 1/2 fl oz) Absolut Citron
20 ml (^{1}/3 fl oz) triple sec
20 ml (^{2}/3 fl oz) cranberry juice
juice of ^{1}/2 fresh Lime

Pour ingredients into a cocktail shaker over ice and shake.
Strain into chilled glass.

Bermuda Rose

Glass: martini
Garnish: slice of lime

30 ml (1 fl oz) gin
10 ml (^{1}/3 fl oz) lime juice
1 teaspoon grenadine
4–5 drops of apricot brandy

Pour ingredients into a cocktail shaker over ice and shake.
Strain into chilled glass.

Between the Sheets

Glass: coupe
Garnish: lemon slice and twist

30 ml (1 fl oz) brandy
30 ml (1 fl oz) Bacardi
30 ml (1 fl oz) Cointreau
15 ml (½ fl oz) lemon juice

Pour ingredients into a cocktail shaker over ice and shake.
Strain into chilled glass.

Blue Bayou

Glass: highball
Garnish: mint sprig and lemon wheel

15 ml (1/2 fl oz) vanilla Galliano
15 ml (1/2 fl oz) dry vermouth
30 ml (1 fl oz) gin
15 ml (1/2 fl oz) blue curaçao
lemonade, to top

Pour ingredients into a cocktail shaker over ice and shake.
Strain over fresh ice.

Brandy Alexander

Glass: coupe
Garnish: nutmeg sprinkle

30 ml (1 fl oz) brandy
30 ml (1 fl oz) dark crème de cacao
30 ml (1 fl oz) cream

Pour ingredients into a cocktail shaker over ice and shake.
Double strain into chilled glass.

Cherries Jubilee

Glass: martini
Garnish: grated chocolate and cherry on rim of glass

30 ml (1 fl oz) cherry advocaat
30 ml (1 fl oz) white crème de cacao
15 ml (1/2 fl oz) Malibu
40 ml (1 1/3 fl oz) cream
15 ml (1/2 fl oz) milk

Pour ingredients into a cocktail shaker over ice and shake.
Double strain into chilled glass.

Espresso Martini

Glass: martini
Garnish: 3 coffee beans

> 30 ml freshly brewed espresso coffee
> 30 ml vodka
> 30 ml Kahlua
> 5 ml sugar syrup (optional)

Pour ingredients into a cocktail shaker over ice and shake vigorously. Double strain into chilled glass.

> Mixture must be shaken hard and strained/ poured immediately to create the crema that sits on top of the cocktail.

Variations
Frangelico: Replace Kahlua with 30 ml Frangelico.

Vanilla: Either replace vodka with vanilla vodka, or use the following proportions: 30 ml fresh espresso, 20 ml vodka, 20 ml Kahlua, 20 ml vanilla Galliano.

Salted caramel: Replace half the Kahlua with 15 ml vanilla Galliano. Replace sugar syrup with 15 ml salted caramel syrup.

Rum: Replace vodka with spiced rum.

Irish: Replace vodka with Jamesons.

Geisha

Glass: champagne flute
Garnish: cherry

> 30 ml (1 fl oz) bourbon
> 30 ml (1 fl oz) sake
> 10 1/3 fl oz) lemon juice
> 10 ml (1/3fl oz) sugar syrup

Pour ingredients into a cocktail shaker over ice and shake.
Strain into chilled glass.

Gimlet

Glass: old fashioned or coupe
Garnish: lime wheel

> 60 ml (2 fl oz) gin
> 30 ml (1 fl oz) lime juice
> 15 ml (1/2 fl oz) sugar syrup

Pour ingredients into a cocktail shaker. Shake over ice and pour, then add cubed ice.

This cocktail can also be made using pear juice. Adjust sugar syrup to taste

God Daughter

Glass: coupe
Garnish: flaked chocolate, strawberry and mint

> 30 ml (1 fl oz) vodka
> 30 ml (1 fl oz) Amaretto
> 30 ml (1 fl oz) heavy cream
> 1 teaspoon grenadine

Pour ingredients into a cocktail shaker over ice and shake. Double strain into chilled glass.

Golden Cadillac

Glass: martini
Garnish: red cherry or strawberry

30 ml (1 fl oz) vanilla Galliano
30 ml (1 fl oz) crème de cacao
30 ml (1 fl oz) cream

Pour ingredients into a cocktail shaker over ice and shake.
Double strain into chilled glass.

Golden Dream

Glass: martini
Garnish: chocolate powder rim

30 ml (1 fl oz) vanilla Galliano
20 ml (2/3 fl oz) Cointreau or triple sec
20 ml (2/3 fl oz) orange juice
20 ml (2/3 fl oz) cream

Pour ingredients into a cocktail shaker over ice and shake.
Double strain into chilled glass.

Grasshopper

Glass: coupe
Garnish: shaved chocolate

> 30 ml (1 fl oz) crème de menthe
> 30 ml (1 fl oz) white crème de cacao
> 30 ml (1 fl oz) cream

Pour ingredients into a cocktail shaker over ice and shake.
Double strain into chilled glass.

Some people prefer dark crème de cacao instead
of white crème de cacao.

Green with Envy

Glass: hurricane glass
Garnish: pineapple spear with leaves and cherry.
Serve with straws.

30 ml (1 fl oz) ouzo
30 ml (1 fl oz) blue curaçao
120 ml (4 fl oz) pineapple juice

Pour ingredients into a cocktail shaker over ice and shake.
Strain over fresh ice.

Hawaiian Punch

Glass: hurricane glass
Garnish: orange slice and a cherry

20 ml (2/3 fl oz) Southern Comfort
20 ml (2/3 fl oz) amaretto
15 ml (1/2 fl oz) vodka
40 ml (1 1/3 fl oz) pineapple juice
40 ml (1 1/3 fl oz) orange juice
20 ml (2/3 fl oz) lime juice
20 ml (2/3 fl oz) grenadine, to top

Pour all ingredients except for grenadine into a cocktail
shaker over ice and shake. Strain over fresh ice and gently
tip grenadine in.

Hurricane

Glass: hurricane glass
Garnish: orange slice and cherry

30 ml (1 fl oz) Bacardi
30 ml (1 fl oz) orange juice
15 ml (1/2 fl oz)lime cordial
45 ml (1 1/2 fl oz) lemon juice
45 ml (1 1/2 fl oz) sugar syrup
15 ml Bacardi Gold, to top

Pour all ingredients except for Bacardi Gold into a cocktail shaker over ice and shake.
Strain over fresh ice and gently float Bacardi Gold on top.

Japanese Slipper

Glass: martini
Garnish: slice of lemon on side of glass

> 30 ml (1 fl oz) melon liqueur
> 30 ml (1 fl oz) Cointreau
> 30 ml (1 fl oz) lemon juice

Pour ingredients into a cocktail shaker over ice and shake.
Strain into chilled glass.

Kamikaze

Glass: martini
Garnish: red cocktail onion on a toothpick in the glass

> 30 ml (1 fl oz) vodka
> 30 ml (1 fl oz) Cointreau
> 30 ml (1 fl oz) fresh lemon juice
> 1 teaspoon lime cordial

Pour ingredients into a cocktail shaker over ice and shake.
Strain into chilled glass.

Maintain freshness for larger volumes by adding stained egg white. Mix in a jug and keep refrigerated. Cointreau may be replaced with triple sec.

Kick in the Balls

Glass: martini
Garnish: Two melon balls previously marinated in the rum.

30 ml (1 fl oz) rum
30 ml (1 fl oz) orange juice
30 ml (1 fl oz) melon liqueur
30 ml (1 fl oz) cream
15 ml (1/2 fl oz) coconut cream

Pour ingredients into a cocktail shaker over ice and shake. Double strain into chilled glass.

Lights of Havana

Glass: highball
Garnish: A straw and a lime wheel.

60 ml (2 fl oz) soda water
45 ml (1 1/2 fl oz) Malibu
30 ml (1 fl oz) Midori
60 ml (2 fl oz) orange juice
60 ml (2 fl oz) pineapple juice

Pour all ingredients except for soda water into a cocktail shaker over ice and shake. Strain over fresh ice and top with soda.

Long Island Iced Tea

Glass: highball or hurricane
Garnish: Lemon twist and mint leaves. Serve with straws.

30 ml (1 fl oz) vodka
30 ml (1 fl oz) white rum
30 ml (1 fl oz) Cointreau
30 ml (1 fl oz) tequila
30 ml (1 fl oz) gin
30 ml (1 fl oz) lemon juice
dash of cola
30 ml (1 fl oz) sugar syrup

Pour all ingredients except for cola into a cocktail shaker over ice and shake. Strain over fresh ice and top with cola.

The tea-coloured cola is splashed into the cocktail making it slightly unsuitable for a "tea party". Many variations are concocted using different white spirits. It is strongly recommended that you consume no more than one.

Louisiana Lullaby

Glass: martini
Garnish: A twist of lemon

> 30 ml (1 fl oz) dark rum
> 10 ml (1/3 fl oz) Dubonnet
> 1 teaspoon Grand Marnier

Pour ingredients into a cocktail shaker over ice and shake. Strain into chilled glass.

Madam Butterfly

Glass: margarita
Garnish: strawberry and butterfly

Shaker 1

> 30 ml (1 fl oz) passionfruit liqueur (or 1/2 passionfruit)
> 15 ml (1/2 fl oz) melon liqueur
> 15 ml (1/2 fl oz) white crème de cacao
> 30 ml pineapple juice

Shaker 2

> 30 ml (1 fl oz) cream
> 15 ml (1/2 fl oz) melon liqueur

This cocktail requires two shakers. In one hand, shake the first four ingredients over ice and strain into chilled glass. In the other hand, shake melon liqueur and cream, then strain over the top.

Mai Tai

Glass: highball
Garnish: Pineapple spear, mint leaves, tropical flowers if possible (e.g. Singapore orchid), lime shell. Serve with straws.

30 ml (1 fl oz) rum
15 ml (1/2 fl oz) dark rum
30 ml (1 fl oz) orange curacao
15 ml (1/2 fl oz) Amaretto
30 ml (1 fl oz) sugar syrup
30 ml (1 fl oz) lemon juice
15-30 ml sugar syrup
1/2 fresh lime, juiced

Pour ingredients into a cocktail shaker over ice and shake. Strain over fresh ice.

Grenadine is often added to redden a glowing effect while the rum may be floated on top when served without straws.

Margarita

Glass: margarita
Garnish: lime wheel on edge of glass and salt rim

> 60 ml (2 fl oz) tequila
> 30 ml (1 fl oz) lime juice
> 30 ml (1 fl oz) Cointreau

Pour ingredients into a cocktail shaker over ice and shake.
Strain into chilled glass.

Monkey Gland

Glass: martini
Garnish: plastic monkey

> 30 ml (1 fl oz) gin
> 10 ml (1/3 fl oz) apple juice
> 1 teaspoon Parfait Amour
> 1 teaspoon grenadine

Pour ingredients into a cocktail shaker over ice and shake.
Strain into chilled glass.

Variation:
Substitute 20 ml pernod for the Parfait Amour and
grenadine.

Pago Pago

Glass: old fashioned
Garnish: A pineapple wedge and a cherry

> 30 ml (1 fl oz) Bacardi Gold Rum
> 10 ml (1/3 fl oz) lime juice
> 10 ml (1/3 fl oz) pineapple juice
> 1 teaspoon green Chartreuse
> 1 teaspoon Cointreau

Pour ingredients into a cocktail shaker over ice and shake.
Strain over fresh ice.

Picasso

Glass: coupe
Garnish: An orange twist

> 30 ml (1 fl oz) cognac
> 10 ml (1/3 fl oz) Dubonnet
> 10 ml (1/3 fl oz) lime juice
> 15 ml (1/2 fl oz) sugar syrup

Pour ingredients into a cocktail shaker over ice and shake.
Strain into chilled glass.

Pink Panther

Glass: coupe
Garnish: Cherry and mint.

> 20 ml bourbon
> 30 ml (1 fl oz) vodka
> 15 ml (1/2 fl oz) Malibu
> 40 ml cream
> dash of grenadine

Pour ingredients into a cocktail shaker over ice and shake.
Double strain into chilled glass.

Polish Sidecar

Glass: martini
Garnish: orange twist

> 30 ml (1 fl oz) dark rum
> 30 ml (1 fl oz) lemon or lime juice
> 60 ml (2 fl oz) orange juice
> 1 teaspoon grenadine

Pour all ingredients except for the grenadine into a cocktail
shaker over ice and shake. Strain and gently pour the
grenadine down the inside of the glass.

Quebec

Glass: martini
Garnish: a cocktail onion

> 30 ml (1 fl oz) Canadian Club whisky
> 10 ml (1/3 fl oz) dry vermouth
> 10 ml (1/3 fl oz) Amer Picon
> 10 ml (1/3 fl oz) maraschino liqueur

Pour ingredients into a cocktail shaker over ice and shake. Strain into chilled glass.

> Amer Picon is a French bitters that derives much of its flavour from gentian root and oranges. 3 ml Angostura bitters may be substituted.

Singapore Sling

Glass: hurricane or highball
Garnish: orange slice, mint, a cherry, swizzle stick and straws

> 30 ml (1 fl oz) gin
> 30 ml (1 fl oz) orange juice
> 30 ml (1 fl oz) cherry brandy liqueur
> 30 ml (1 fl oz) lime juice
> 30 ml (1 fl oz) pineapple juice
> 15 ml (1/2 fl oz) triple sec
> 15 ml (1/2 fl oz) Benedictine
> dash Angostura bitters

Pour ingredients into a cocktail shaker over ice and shake. Strain over fresh ice.

Sidecar

Glass: martini
Garnish: lemon twist optional

> 30 ml (1 fl oz) brandy
> 20 ml Cointreau*
> 20 ml lemon juice

Pour ingredients into a cocktail shaker over ice and shake.
Strain into chilled glass.

Cointreau may be substituted with triple sec.

Southern Peach

Glass: martini
Garnish: butterfly a strawberry, place on side of glass, twirl
cream over strawberry and sprinkle flaked chocolate

> 30 ml (1 fl oz) Cointreau
> 15 ml (1/2 fl oz) brandy
> 15 ml (1/2 fl oz) cherry brandy liqueur
> 15 ml (1/2 fl oz) pineapple juice
> 15 ml (1/2 fl oz) lemon juice

Pour ingredients into a cocktail shaker over ice and shake.
Strain into chilled glass.

Sweet Lady Jane

Glass: coupe
Garnish: Strawberry, mint and chocolate flakes

15 ml (1/2 fl oz) Grand Marnier
15 ml (1/2 fl oz) orange juice
15 ml (1/2 fl oz) Cointreau
15 ml (1/2 fl oz) coconut cream
30 ml (1 fl oz) strawberry liqueur
30 ml (1 fl oz) fresh cream

Pour ingredients into a cocktail shaker over ice and shake.
Double strain into chilled glass.

Toblerone

Glass: martini
Garnish: chocolate swirl in glass and nutmeg over top

1 teaspoon Bailey's Irish Cream
15 ml (1/2 fl oz) Kahlúa
15 ml (1/2 fl oz) white crème de cacao
30 ml (1 fl oz) Frangelico
60 ml (2 fl oz) cream
1/2 teaspoon honey

Pour ingredients into a cocktail shaker over ice and shake.
Double strain into chilled glass.

Trader Vic's Rum Fizz

Glass: champagne flute
Garnish: an orange spiral

30 ml (1 fl oz) dark rum
30 ml (1 fl oz) lemon juice
10 ml (1/3 fl oz) sugar
15 ml (1/2 fl oz) creaming soda
1 raw egg

Pour all ingredients except for the creaming soda into a cocktail shaker over ice and shake. Double strain into chilled glass and top with creaming soda.

Whisky Sour

Glass: old fashioned
Garnish: red cherry and slice of lemon

60 ml (1 1/2 fl oz) Scotch whisky
30 ml (1 fl oz) lemon juice
15 ml (1/2 fl oz) sugar syrup
1/2 egg white

Add ingredients to shaker and shake vigorously for 10-15 seconds without ice. Add ice to shaker and shake. Double strain over fresh ice.

Variation:
Amaretto Sour: replace the whisky with Amaretto.

White Lady

Glass: martini
Garnish: twist of lemon

30 ml (1 fl oz) dry gin
15 ml (1/2 fl oz) lemon juice
15 ml (1/2 fl oz) sugar syrup
1/2 egg white

Add ingredients to shaker and shake vigorously for 10-15 seconds without ice. Add ice to shaker and shake. Double strain into a chilled glass.

Widow's Kiss

Glass: martini
Garnish: a floating strawberry

30 ml (1 fl oz) apple brandy
10 ml (1/3 fl oz) Benedictine
10 ml (1/3 fl oz) yellow chartreuse
1 teaspoon Angostura bitters

Pour ingredients into a cocktail shaker over ice and shake. Double strain into chilled glass.

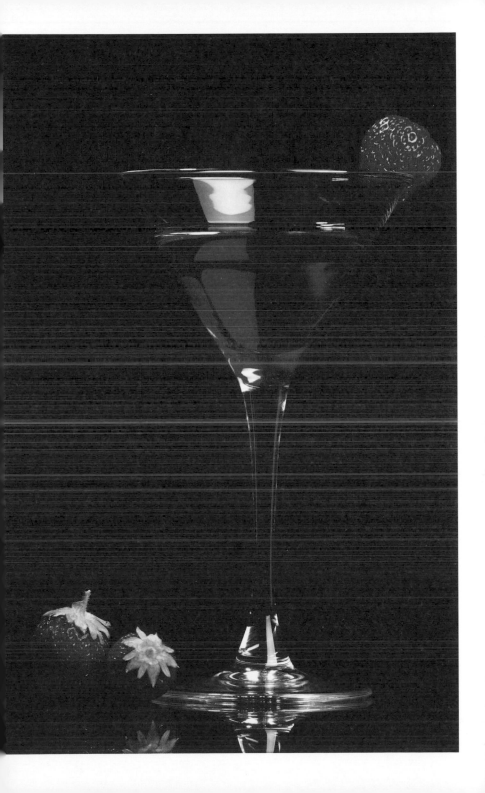

Woodstock

Glass: martini or coupe
Garnish: sugar rimmed with maple syrup

30 ml (1 fl oz) gin
10 ml (1/3 fl oz) lemon juice
10 ml (1/3 fl oz) maple syrup
2 dashes Angostura bitters

Pour ingredients into a cocktail shaker over ice and shake.
Double strain into chilled glass.

XTC

Glass: martini
Garnish: butterfly strawberry placed on side of glass, twirl
thickened cream over strawberry and sprinkle over flaked
chocolate

30 ml (1 fl oz) Tia Maria
30 ml (1 fl oz) strawberry liqueur
30 ml (1 fl oz) cream

Pour ingredients into a cocktail shaker over ice and shake.
Double strain into chilled glass.

Zombie

Glass: highball
Garnish: pineapple spear and leaves, mint leaves and cherry, swizzle stick and straws

40 ml Bacardi
30 ml (1 fl oz) dark rum
30 ml (1 fl oz) light rum
30 ml (1 fl oz) pineapple juice
15 ml (1/2 fl oz) lime or lemon juice
30 ml (1 fl oz) apricot brandy
1 teaspoon sugar syrup

Pour ingredients into a cocktail shaker over ice and shake. Strain over fresh ice.

Stir

Strong, bold, and always delicious.

Dry Martini

Glass: martini
Garnish: green olive

> 60 ml (2 oz) dry gin
> 10-15 ml (1/3-1/2 oz) dry vermouth

Pour gin and vermouth into a mixing glass over ice then stir until liquid is chilled. Strain into a chilled martini glass, add olive then serve.

Variations
Gibson: replace olive with white cocktail onion

Martini on the Rocks: Stir and strain over ice in a rocks glass.

Racquet Club Martini: add two dashes of orange bitters, garnish with orange twist instead of olive.

Smoky Martini: replace vermouth with a couple of dashes of peated Scotch whiskey, garnish with lemon twist instead of olive.

Martini Oriental: replace vermouth with 15 ml (1/2 fl oz) sake, garnish with lemon twist instead of olive.

Chambord Martini: replace vermouth with 30 ml (1 fl oz) Chambord, garnish with lemon twist insead of olive.

Gunga Din Martini: add 23 ml (3/4 fl oz) orange juice, garnish with a wedge of fresh pineapple.

Sweet Martini: replace dry vermouth with 30 ml (1 fl oz) of sweet vermouth, garnish with a maraschino cherry.

Dirty Martini: Add 15 ml (1/2 fl oz) olive brine before stirring.

Perfect Martini

Glass: martini
Garnish: lemon twist

30 ml (1 oz) dry gin
15 ml (1/2 oz) dry vermouth
15 ml (1/2 oz) sweet vermouth

Pour ingredients into a mixing glass over ice and stir gently until liquid is chilled. Strain into a chilled martini glass and serve.

This is a variation of a Perfect Manhattan, using vodka as the base spirit.

Vodka Martini

Glass: martini
Garnish: lemon twist

60 ml (2 fl oz) vodka
15 ml (1/2 fl oz) dry vermouth

Pour vodka and vermouth into a mixing glass over ice then stir until liquid is chilled. Strain into a chilled martini glass and garnish with a twist of lemon peel then serve.

Variations:
Sweet Vodka Martini: replace dry vermouth with 30 ml (1 fl oz) sweet vermouth.

Peach Vodka Martini: replace vermouth with 30 ml (1 fl oz) peach schnapps.

Hazelnut Vodka Martini: replace vermouth with 30 ml (1 fl oz) Frangelico.

Blue Martini

Glass: martini
Garnish: single blueberry on rim of glass

45 ml (11/2 fl oz) vodka
10 ml (2/3 fl oz) blue curaçao
10 ml (2/3 fl oz) fresh lemon juice
4 fresh blueberries (diced)

Place diced blueberries into a mixing glass without ice and muddle well then add ice. Add vodka, curaçao and juice then stir well to combine the ingredients. Double strain into a chilled martini glass and garnish with a blueberry then serve.

Comfortable Martini

Glass: martini
Garnish: lemon twist

60 ml (2 oz) honey vodka
15 ml (1/2 oz) Southern Comfort

Pour ingredients into a mixing glass over ice and stir until chilled. Strain into a chilled cocktail glass, garnish with lemon twist and serve.

Bellini Martini

Glass: brandy balloon
Garnish: lemon twist

> 60 ml (2 oz) vodka
> 30 ml (1 oz) peach schnapps
> 30 ml (1 oz) peach nectar

Pour vodka, schnapps and nectar into a mixing glass over ice and stir well. Strain into a chilled brandy balloon and add a twist of lemon peel then serve.

French Martini

Glass: martini
Garnish: pineapple wedge

> 45 ml (11/2 oz) vodka
> 30 ml (1 oz) black raspberry liqueur
> 30 ml (1 fl oz) pineapple juice

Pour ingredients into a mixing glass over ice and stir until chilled. Strain into a chilled martini glass and serve.

Bloody Mary

Glass: highball
Garnish: celery stalk, lemon slice

> 60 ml (2 fl oz) vodka
> 120 ml (4 fl oz) tomato juice
> salt and pepper to taste
> Worcestershire sauce to taste
> celery salt, optional
> Tabasco sauce to taste
> lemon juice to taste

Pour ingredients into a mixing glass over ice and stir. Strain into glass and serve.

Remember to add the spices first, then vodka and lemon juice followed by tomato juice. The celery stick is not just part of the garnish, so feel free to nibble as you drink. The glass may also be salt-rimmed. Feel free to play around with the garnish, suggestions include cucumber, olives, cherry tomatoes — anything you like!

Variations:
Virgin Mary: remove the vodka from the recipe, so it is non-alcoholic.

Bloody Maria: replace the vodka with 60 ml (2 fl oz) tequila

Blue Hawaii

Glass: small highball
Garnish: pineapple wedge and half strawberry

30 ml (1 fl oz) Bacardi
30 ml (1 fl oz) blue curaçao
60 ml (2 fl oz) pineapple juice
30 ml (1 fl oz) lemon juice
30 ml (1 fl oz) sugar syrup

Pour ingredients into a mixing glass over ice and stir until chilled. Strain into glass and serve.

Dizzy Blonde

Glass: highball
Garnish: cherry and orange slice

60 ml (2 fl oz) advocaat
30 ml (1 fl oz) Pernod
chilled lemonade, to top

Stir advocaat and Pernot together. Top with lemonade while stirring.

GRB

Glass: small martini glass
Garnish: mint leaf floated on top

> 30 ml (1 fl oz) vanilla Galliano
> 10 ml (1/3 fl oz) grenadine
> 30 ml (1 fl oz) dark rum

Pour ingredients into a mixing glass with ice and stir. Strain into glass and serve. The mint infuses with the rum to mellow it as you drink.

Manhattan

Glass: martini
Garnish: A red cherry on toothpick in glass

> 60 ml (2 fl oz) rye whiskey
> 30 ml (1 fl oz) sweet vermouth
> dash Angostura bitters

Stir over ice until chilled. Strain into a chilled glass.

Variations:
Dry Manhattan: replace sweet vermouth with dry vermouth and add a twist of lemon.

Perfect Manhattan: replace half the sweet vermouth with dry vermouth.

Mint Julep

Glass: old fashioned
Garnish: mint

60 ml (2 fl oz) bourbon
10 ml (1/3 fl oz) sugar syrup
2–3 dashes cold water or soda water
8 sprigs of fresh mint
crushed or shaved ice

Muddle sugar syrup and 5 mint sprigs in a glass until the mint becomes fragrant, but stop before it breaks up. Pour into thoroughly frosted glass and pack with ice. Add bourbon and water/soda and mix (with a chopping motion using a long-handled bar spoon). Garnish with remaining mint and serve with a straw.

Montmatre

Glass: martini
Garnish: red cherry on side of glass

10 ml (1/3 fl oz) Cointreau
30 ml (1 fl oz) gin
10 ml (1/3 fl oz) sweet vermouth

Coat glass with Cointreau then pour gin and sweet vermouth over ice.

From the world-renowned painters courtyard next to the Sacré Coeur overlooking Paris.

Negroni

Glass: old fashioned
Garnish: twist of orange peel and an oversized ice cube

> 20 ml (2/3 fl oz) **Campari**
> 20 ml (2/3 fl oz) **sweet vermouth**
> 20 ml (2/3 fl oz) **gin**

Pour ingredients into mixing glass and stir until chilled.
Strain over oversized ice cube. Squeeze orange peel over
glass to release the oils before dropping it in.

Variations:
Boulevardier: replace gin with rye whiskey

Old Fashioned

Glass: old fashioned
Garnish: twist of orange peel, cherry, and an oversized ice cube

> 60 ml (2 fl oz) bourbon or rye whiskey
> 2 dashes bitters
> sugar cube

Place sugar cube in glass, coat with bitters and muddle. Add whiskey and stir until sugar is completely dissolved. Add oversized ice cube and squeeze orange peel over the glass to release the oils before dropping in the drink.

Variations:
Rum Old Fashioned: replace bourbon/rye with 60 ml (2 fl oz) brown rum

Ole

Glass: small martini glass
Garnish: lemon wheel

> 30 ml (1 fl oz) tequila
> 30 ml (1 fl oz) banana liqueur
> 10 ml (1/3 fl oz) blue curaçao

Stir the tequila and banana liqueur gently over ice to avoid 'bruising' and strain into the glass, then drop blue curaçao.

P.S I Love You

Glass: coupe
Garnish: sprinkled nutmeg

> 30 ml (1 fl oz) Amaretto
> 30 ml (1 fl oz) Kahlúa
> 30 ml (1 fl oz) Bailey's Irish Cream
> 1 teaspoon grenadine

Build over ice and stir.

Sangria

Glass: wine glass
Garnish: none

> 20 ml (2/3 fl oz) Cointreau
> 20 ml (2/3 fl oz) brandy
> 20 ml (2/3 fl oz) Bacardi
> orange, lime, lemon and strawberry pieces, berries
> 20 ml (2/3 fl oz) sugar syrup
> 90 ml (3 fl oz) red wine

Pour in order. Thinly slice orange, lemon and lime, chop strawberries and place in bowl. Pour in sugar syrup and allow to stand for several hours. Add red wine.

Shanghai Punch

Glass: glass coffee cup
Garnish: none

> 30 ml (1 fl oz) cognac
> 30 ml (1 fl oz) dark rum
> 45 ml (1 1/2 fl oz) orange juice
> 20 ml (2/3 fl oz) Cointreau
> 20 ml (2/3 fl oz) lemon juice
> almond extract
> fresh tea
> grated orange and lemon peel
> cinnamon stick

Boil tea and add ingredients then stir.

Try using different flavored teas with this recipe.

Stinger

Glass: small martini
Garnish: none

45 ml (1 1/2 fl oz) brandy
10 ml (1/3 fl oz) white crème de menthe

Stir over ice and strain.

Sunken Treasure

Glass: martini
Garnish: place a teaspoon of apricot conserve in the bottom
of glass and then push a strawberry into conserve

30 ml (1 fl oz) gin
15 ml (1/2 fl oz) peach liqueur
champagne to top up
apricot conserve

Stir over ice, strain and top up with champagne.

TNT

Glass: martini
Garnish: orange twist

45 ml (1 1/2 fl oz) brandy
20 ml (2/3 fl oz) orange liqueur
dash of Pernod
dash of Angostura bitters

Stir over ice and strain.

Tom Collins

Glass: highball
Garnish: serve with a slice of lemon and cherry

30 ml (2 fl oz) lemon juice
60 ml (2 fl oz) gin
15 ml (1/2 fl oz) sugar syrup
soda water

Put cracked ice, lemon juice, and gin in
a glass. Fill with soda water and stir.

Index of cocktails